Cookbook

Kathleen Stang

**ILLUSTRATED BY
JOHN LAVIN**

A LITTLE
Northwest Cookbook

Kathleen Stang

ILLUSTRATED BY
JOHN LAVIN

Chronicle Books

First published in 1993 by
Appletree Press Ltd.
19—21 Alfred Street, Belfast BT2 8DL
Tel. +44 232 243074 Fax +44 232 246756
© Copyright Appletree Press Ltd.
Printed in the E.C. All rights reserved.
No part of this publication may be
reproduced or transmitted in any form or
by any means, electronic or mechanical,
photocopying, recording or any information
and retrieval system, without permission
in writing from Appletree Press Ltd.

First published in the United States in 1993
by Chronicle Books, 275 Fifth Street,
San Francisco, California 94103

ISBN 0-8118-0356-2

9 8 7 6 5 4 3 2 1

Introduction

The Northwest of America – the states of Oregon, Washington, Idaho and Alaska and the Canadian province of British Columbia – offers a cornucopia of food choices. The impressive bounty encompasses fresh-caught salmon and Dungeness crab, pristine shellfish, asparagus and sweet Walla Walla onions, wild mushrooms, blackberries and strawberries too fragile to travel, more than a hundred varieties of apples, pears, and nuts (especially hazelnuts), great coffee, beer, and world-class wines.

There is a patriotic pride for our local ingredients here in the northwest corner of the continent. We tend to use regional foods when possible, promote our native wine industry and patronize our local producers and many farmers' markets, from Seattle's 85-year-old Pike Place Market to Vancouver's Granville Island.

The cuisine of the Pacific Northwest has been shaped by our appreciation for superb local ingredients – particularly seafood, orchard fruit, berries, and wild mushrooms – and enhanced by the influence of immigrant groups and Native Americans as well as the close proximity to the Pacific Rim Countries.

What follows is a sampler of recipes showcasing the many fine Northwest ingredients.

A note on measures

Spoon measurements are level except where otherwise indicated. Seasonings can of course be adjusted according to taste. Recipes are for four, unless otherwise noted.

3

Cranberry-Lemon Scones

Fresh buttered scones with raspberry jam are part of "doing" the Western Washington State Fair in Puyallup. Light and flaky, these scones are dotted with dried cranberries – a Northwest product from the boggy areas near the coast. If you can't find dried cranberries, substitute dried cherries or currants.

---

2 cups all-purpose flour	$1/2$ cup dried cranberries
$1/4$ cup sugar	2 tsp grated lemon peel
2 tsp baking powder	$2/3$ cup buttermilk
$1/2$ tsp salt	2 tsp milk
6 tbsp chilled butter	

(makes 8)

Preheat the oven to 425°F. Stir the dry ingredients together in a bowl. Cut in the butter until crumbly. Stir in the dried cranberries and lemon peel. Pour in the buttermilk and stir with a fork until mixture holds together. Gather the soft dough into a ball and gently knead a few times on a floured surface. Pat out dough to an 8-inch circle and cut into 8 wedges. Place 2 inches apart on a greased baking sheet and brush the tops with milk. Bake 15 minutes or until golden. Serve warm.

Peach Dutch Baby

The Dutch Baby, a puffy German pancake, gained fame at a Seattle restaurant many years ago. Powdered sugar and a squeeze of fresh lemon are the classic topping, but when fresh local peaches are in season, there is nothing better.

Pancake:	Peach Topping:
4 tbsp butter	3 ripe peaches
4 eggs	1–2 tbsp butter
1 cup milk	1 tsp vanilla
1 cup all-purpose flour	1–2 tbsp packed brown sugar
1/2 tsp salt	1/4 tsp cinnamon

Preheat the oven to 425°F. Place the butter in a large heavy oven-proof skillet and place in the oven. While the butter melts, blend the eggs and milk in a food processor or blender. Stir together the flour and salt and sprinkle over the milk mixture. Blend just until smooth. When the butter bubbles, remove the pan from the oven and swirl to coat the side. Pour in the batter. Bake 20 minutes or until puffy and golden brown.

Meanwhile, peel and slice the peaches. Sauté them in the butter in another skillet. Add the vanilla, brown sugar and cinnamon and cook until tender. Spoon the warm peaches into the cooked pancake. Serve warm.

Norwegian Potato Pancakes

In Seattle's Scandinavian neighborhood of Ballard, some Norwegian immigrants fill their lefse, the thin potato pancakes, with ludefisk, lye-soaked fish. But it is more common to butter the lefse and sprinkle them with cinnamon sugar to serve as a snack with a cup of coffee. They are particularly popular during the Christmas holidays and the May 17th Norwegian Independence Day celebration.

1 ½ lb Russet baking potatoes, peeled and diced	1 cup all-purpose flour, plus extra for rolling
3 tbsp milk	vegetable oil
butter	cinnamon sugar
¾ tsp salt	
(makes 12)	

Boil the potatoes in water to cover until tender. Drain, then mash until very smooth, to make about 3 cups. Stir in the milk, 1 ½ tbsp butter and salt; cool. Mix in the flour to make a soft, non-sticky dough. Knead gently and shape into a log. Cut into 12 pieces. Roll out each piece on a floured cloth to a thin, 9-inch round. Transfer the lefse to a piece of floured plastic wrap, dust with flour and stack. (Some Norwegians roll out the next lefse while the previous one is cooking.)

Heat a heavy griddle over medium heat and lightly coat with oil. Brush excess flour off 1 lefse and cook about 1 ½ minutes per side or until blistered and lightly brown. Transfer to a warm dish and keep warm while cooking remaining lefse. Spread the lefse with butter and sprinkle with cinnamon sugar. Fold into quarters and serve warm.

Pork Hum Bao

Vancouver's Chinatown, the second largest in North America, is particularly lively on Sundays. Baked pork-filled buns – hum bao – and hot tea make a great snack and are also served as part of the traditional Dim Sum meal.

2 tbsp sherry or water	³/₄ cup sliced green onion
4 tsp soy sauce	¹/₃ cup hoisin sauce
2 tsp cornstarch	1 lb loaf frozen yeast bread
1 clove garlic, minced	dough, thawed
1 ¹/₂ cups diced lean pork	1 egg yolk beaten with 1 tsp
1 tbsp peanut oil	water

(makes 16)

Combine the sherry, soy sauce, cornstarch and garlic in a bowl. Stir in the pork and set aside for 15 minutes. Heat the oil in a skillet or wok. Add the green onion and stir-fry 1 minute. Add the pork mixture and continue to stir-fry about 3 minutes or until cooked through. Reduce the heat, stir in the hoisin sauce and simmer 5 minutes. Cool.

Cut the bread dough into 16 equal pieces and flatten each to a 3-inch circle. Divide the meat filling among the circles and pull the dough up around the filling to make a ball. Pinch together to seal and place, seam side down, 2 inches apart, on a baking sheet lined with parchment paper. Cover with a tea towel and let rise in a warm place 45 minutes or until puffy. Preheat oven to 350°F. Brush the buns with egg mixture. Bake 15 minutes or until golden brown. Serve warm.

Sheepherder's Bread

In the Basque region of Idaho, Sheepherder's Bread was traditionally leavened with sourdough starter and baked in a big cast-iron Dutch oven covered with coals. This version is far less complicated. Beer replaces the starter and the bread is shaped in a 3-quart cast-iron chicken fryer (the kind with a glass lid) – or other heavy pan – and baked in a conventional oven.

---

5 ¹/₂–6 cups bread flour, plus extra for kneading	1 ¹/₂ tsp salt
	1 ¹/₂ cups beer
2 packages dry yeast	¹/₂ cup water
3 tbsp sugar	2 tbsp vegetable oil

(makes 1 large 10-inch round loaf)

Stir together 2 cups flour, yeast, sugar, and salt in the large bowl of an electric mixer. Heat the beer and water until very warm (120°F–130°F). Add with the oil to the flour mixture and beat at medium speed until smooth. Stir in enough of remaining flour to make a stiff dough. Turn out onto a floured surface and knead 12 to 15 minutes until smooth and elastic. Place in a large greased bowl. Cover and let rise in a warm place (80°F–85°F) until double, about 1 hour. Meanwhile, thoroughly oil a 3-quart cast-iron chicken fryer and the inside of the lid. Punch down the dough, knead a few minutes on a floured surface, and form into a ball. Place in the pan, oil the top and cover with the lid. Let rise in a warm place about 1 hour or until dough pushes up the lid by 1 inch. Meanwhile, preheat the oven to 375°F.

Bake, with the lid on, 12 minutes. Remove the lid and continue to bake for a total of 55 to 65 minutes. Remove from the pan and cool on a rack.

Cheddar Beer Soup

Microbreweries and brew pubs are multiplying throughout the Northwest. Brewers are attracted to the area because of the good water and the locally grown hops. For this tangy soup, choose a sharp Cheddar such as Tillamook, from the lush Oregon coast. Tillamook is an Indian word for "land of many waters".

1 onion, diced	1 $^3/_4$–2 cups chicken broth
2 tbsp butter	$^1/_2$ cup beer
2 tbsp all-purpose flour	1 cup milk
1 Russet baking potato, peeled and diced	$^1/_4$ tsp freshly ground pepper
	1 $^1/_4$ cups shredded sharp Cheddar cheese

Sauté the onion in butter in a large saucepan until soft. Add the flour and sauté 1 minute. Gradually stir in the chicken broth and add the potato. Bring to a boil, then simmer, covered, 15 minutes, or until the vegetables are tender. Add the beer and simmer gently 5 minutes. Add the milk and pepper and just heat through without boiling. Remove the pan from the heat and add 1 cup of cheese. Cover the pan and allow to stand 5 minutes or until the cheese is partially melted. Ladle into shallow bowls and sprinkle with the remaining cheese.

Oyster Stew

James Beard, the great food writer and teacher, was passionate about American food, particularly food from his native Northwest. This recipe – using Pacific oysters or the tiny and expensive Olympias – was inspired by his version of oyster stew.

I pt shucked extra small or yearling oysters, drained and liquor reserved	3–4 tbsp butter
	salt
2 cups whole milk	freshly ground pepper
I cup heavy cream	¹/₂–I tsp paprika

Heat 4 soup bowls. Combine the milk, cream, and oyster liquor in a heavy saucepan. Cook over medium heat until just scalding. Meanwhile melt 2 tablespoons of the butter in a large skillet. Add the oysters and cook over moderate heat 2 to 3 minutes or until the edges begin to curl. Pour the hot milk mixture over the oysters and season with salt, pepper and paprika. Place a pat of the remaining butter in each bowl. Ladle the hot stew into the bowls.

Mussels Steamed in Wine

Penn Cove, located on the Puget Sound side of Whidbey Island, is the primary mussel-growing region in the Northwest. It provides small, blue-black aquacultured mussels almost year round. Steamed mussels make an enticing first course served with good sourdough bread and a dry Northwest wine. Double the recipe to use as a main course.

2 lb mussels	2 tsp minced fresh ginger
1 ½ cups dry white wine	1 clove garlic, minced
2 tbsp butter	freshly ground pepper to taste
or olive oil	2 tbsp minced parsley
2 tbsp finely chopped onion	

Rinse the mussels and remove beards. Discard any partially open mussels that do not close when the shell is tapped. Place remaining ingredients, except parsley, in a large saucepan. Bring to a boil. Reduce heat and simmer 5 minutes. Add the mussels, cover and steam for 3 minutes. Stir the mixture and steam until the shells open. Discard any mussels that do not open. Serve the mussels and broth in shallow bowls and scatter with parsley.

Washington Waldorf

Fresh, thinly sliced local asparagus, crisp red apples, and toasted walnuts give this version of Waldorf salad a Northwestern slant. Asparagus thrives in the rich volcanic soil of the Yakima Valley east of the Cascades Mountains.

---

³/₄ lb asparagus	¹/₂–1 tsp honey
2 medium-size red apples	red-leaf lettuce
¹/₄ cup dried cranberries	3 tbsp coarsely chopped
or raisins	walnuts, toasted
¹/₂ cup mayonnaise	

Break off and discard the tough stems of the asparagus and thinly slice on the diagonal. Core and dice the apples and combine with the asparagus and dried cranberries in a bowl. Mix together the mayonnaise and honey and toss with the salad. Line a serving bowl with the lettuce and spoon in the apple mixture. Sprinkle the walnuts on top.

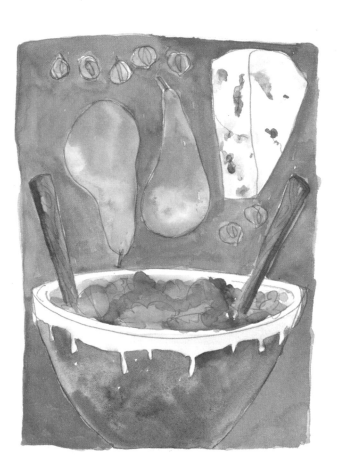

Oregon Blue Cheese and Pear Salad
with Hazelnuts

Three Oregon specialties – fresh pears, hazelnuts (also known as filberts) and blue cheese – combine to make this first-course salad. We like Oregon Blue Cheese from a small creamery in the Rogue River Valley. Depending on the season, choose either summer Bartlett pears or winter Bosc, Anjou, or the dribble-down-the-chin juicy Comice.

3 tbsp hazelnuts
2 tbsp vegetable oil
2 tbsp hazelnut oil or additional vegetable oil
1 tbsp white wine vinegar
1 1/2 tsp lemon juice
1/4 tsp Dijon-style mustard
salt and freshly ground pepper
2 pears
1/4 cup crumbled blue cheese
6 cups mixed greens, such as romaine, spinach and endive

Preheat the oven to 325°F. Toast the hazelnuts about 10 minutes, shaking occasionally. Rub the nuts in a tea towel to remove the loose husks and coarsely chop.

To make the dressing, combine the oils, vinegar, lemon juice, mustard, and salt and pepper to taste in a tightly capped jar and shake vigorously.

Core and dice the pears and combine with salad greens, blue cheese and hazelnuts in a large salad bowl. Shake the dressing again and pour over the salad. Toss and serve.

Lentil and Summer Vegetable Salad

Virtually the entire U. S. crop of lentils is grown in the vast Palouse region of Eastern Washington and Northern Idaho. Further south and west, in Wapato, Washington, are the Krueger Pepper Gardens, growers of more than 60 kinds of peppers.

³/₄ cup lentils, rinsed	¹/₂ cup thinly sliced red onion
I onion, halved	¹/₂ cup minced parsley
I clove garlic, peeled	¹/₄ cup olive oil
I bay leaf	3 tbsp lemon juice
4 cups water	¹/₂ tsp Dijon-style mustard
2 large bell peppers,	³/₄ tsp minced fresh oregano
I red, I yellow	or ¹/₄ tsp dried
I cup cherry tomatoes,	¹/₂ tsp salt
halved if large	freshly ground pepper to taste

Combine the lentils, onions, garlic, bay leaf, and water in a large saucepan. Bring to a boil, reduce the heat and simmer 15 to 20 minutes or just until tender.

Meanwhile, broil the peppers 4 inches from the heat, turning frequently, for about 15 minutes. Place them in a paper bag to steam for 15 minutes. Peel, core and seed the peppers; cut into I x ¹/₄-inch strips. Drain the lentils and discard the onion, garlic, and bay leaf. Toss the warm lentils with the peppers, tomatoes, sliced onion, and parsley in a large bowl. Combine remaining ingredients in a tightly capped jar. Shake well and toss with the salad. Serve warm or at room temperature.

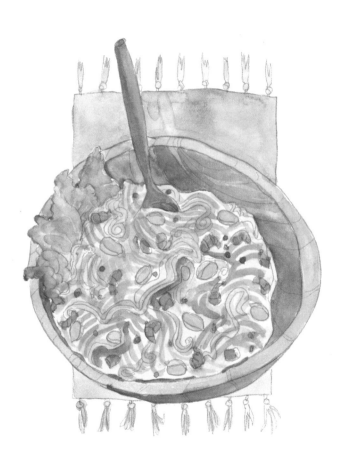

Asian Cold Noodle Salad with Shrimp

Tiny Oregon bay shrimp are sold peeled, cooked and ready to eat — the ultimate convenience food for soups, sandwiches, and summer salads. This recipe pairs a Pacific Rim influence with local ingredients.

---

8 oz somen wheat noodles or vermicelli	6 tbsp rice vinegar
3/4–1 lb cooked small shrimp	1/4 cup low-sodium soy sauce
1 carrot, shredded	2 tbsp vegetable oil
1 zucchini, shredded	1 tbsp sesame oil
2 green onions, thinly sliced on the diagonal	1 tsp sugar
1 tbsp toasted sesame seeds	1/8 tsp hot red pepper flakes
1 tsp minced fresh ginger	1/2 cup chopped peanuts
	small lettuce leaves

(makes about 6 1/2 cups)

Cook the noodles in boiling water about 3 minutes or just until tender. Drain, rinse in cold water and drain again. Place in a large bowl. Add the shrimp, carrot, zucchini, green onion, sesame seeds, and ginger; toss. Combine the vinegar, soy sauce, oils, sugar, and pepper flakes in a tightly capped jar. Shake well, pour over the salad and toss gently. Chill until served. Garnish with the peanuts and lettuce.

Grilled Salmon and Walla Walla Sweets

Salmon is the quintessential seafood of the Pacific Northwest. It was a vital food source for the coastal Indians who roasted it whole in leaf-lined pits and grilled fillets on split-bough frames. For this recipe, choose Chinook (also known as King), silver (Coho) or deep red sockeye steaks to team with Walla Walla sweet onions.

1/4 cup melted butter
2 tbsp lemon juice
1/2 tsp fresh or dried dill
4 (6–8oz each) salmon steaks, about 1 inch thick
salt
freshly ground pepper

2 Walla Walla sweet onions, sliced 3/4 inch thick
oil
lemon wedges

Combine the butter, lemon juice, and dill in a shallow dish. Season the salmon with salt and pepper and arrange in the dish with the onions, coating both sides. Marinate 1/2 hour at room temperature or up to 4 hours in the refrigerator. (Butter will solidify.)

Prepare a barbecue fire and place the grilling rack 4–6 inches from the heat. Brush the hot grill with oil and place the salmon and onions on the grill, reserving the marinade. Grill the fish and onions, turning once and brushing with marinade, 8–10 minutes or until fish just begins to flake. Transfer to a platter and garnish with lemon wedges.

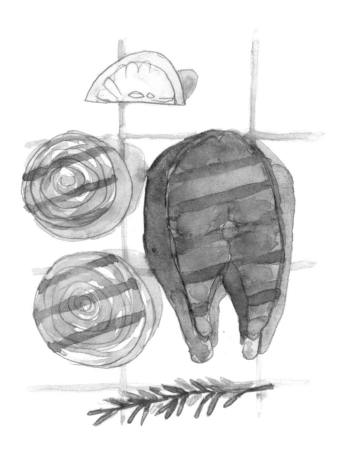

Kate's Christmas Crab

Succulent Dungeness crab, named after a small coastal town on the Olympic Peninsula, comes from the waters off Northern California up to the Aleutian Islands. The larger crabs, about 3 1/2 pounds each, come from Alaska. Although fresh crab is available most of the year, this hearty stew is a winter dish. My friend Kate Nelson serves it on Christmas Eve or Day. Be prepared with lots of napkins; it's messy to eat.

1/4 cup olive oil	1 tbsp white wine vinegar
2 onions, thinly sliced	1 1/2 tsp paprika
1 clove garlic, minced	1/2 tsp turmeric
2 cups dry red wine	1/2 tsp ground ginger
1 1/2 cups tomato juice	1/4 tsp dried thyme
3 tbsp sugar	1/4 tsp hot pepper sauce
4 strips lemon peel	2 cooked Dungeness crabs,
2 tbsp lemon juice	cleaned and cracked
2 tbsp soy sauce	

Heat the oil in a large pan. Add the onions and garlic and sauté until soft. Add the remaining ingredients except the crab. Cover and simmer 1 hour. Preheat the oven to 350°F. Place the crab in a large baking dish and pour the sauce over the top. Cover and bake 30 minutes or until the sauce is bubbly and crab is heated through. Spoon the crab and sauce into shallow bowls.

Clam Spaghetti

This simple dish was the reward after hunting razor clams with one of my sisters near Kenai, Alaska. My nieces and nephews were quick to spot the dimples and fast enough to catch the descending clams. Butter clams or the giant geoduck (gooey-duck) can be substituted. Shuck or steam open the clams, reserve the juice and coarsely chop the clams. Or, use 2 cans of chopped clams (about 6 $\frac{1}{2}$ oz each), including the liquid.

$\frac{1}{4}$ cup olive oil	about 1 cup clam juice
1 large onion, chopped	1 cup chopped clams
1–2 cloves garlic, minced	12 oz spaghetti
$\frac{1}{4}$ tsp hot red pepper flakes	freshly ground pepper
3 tbsp Pesto Sauce	freshly grated Parmesan
(see p. 35)	cheese

Heat the oil in a large skillet over medium heat. Add the onion, garlic and pepper flakes. Sauté slowly about 10 minutes or until the onion is soft. Add the pesto sauce and clam juice; cook, stirring occasionally, about 10 minutes or until slightly reduced. Meanwhile, cook the spaghetti until al dente and keep warm. Add the clams to the skillet and simmer 1 to 2 minutes longer or until the sauce bubbles. Season with pepper and serve over the hot spaghetti. Pass the Parmesan cheese at the table.

Pike Place Market Pesto Sauce

When Pasqualina Verdi started selling homegrown basil at the colorful Pike Place Market nearly 20 years ago, many Seattleites were unfamiliar with the herb and its possibilities. Now the Verdis sell basil by the crate. Pesto is great tossed with any hot pasta, spread over salmon before grilling or drizzled over sliced sun-warmed tomatoes.

---

2 cups (about 2 oz) fresh basil leaves, packed
$1/4$ cup flat-leaf parsley
1–3 cloves garlic, chopped, optional
$1/3 - 1/2$ cup olive oil, plus extra for top
2 tbsp pine nuts, optional
$1/4$ cup freshly grated Parmesan cheese, optional
(makes about $1/2$ cup)

Place basil, parsley, and garlic in the workbowl of a food processor. With the motor running, gradually pour in the oil through the feeder tube. Continue to process until smooth, scraping down the workbowl with a rubber spatula as necessary. Add the pine nuts and/or Parmesan cheese if desired with a little more olive oil and process again. Spoon into a small jar and cover with about $1/4$ inch olive oil to keep the pesto from darkening. Refrigerate or freeze for longer storage.

Chicken with Apples and Fresh Herbs

This quick, low-calorie entrée is a natural after a visit to The Herbfarm in Fall City east of Seattle or the Nichols Garden Nursery in Oregon's Willamette Valley. Use a combination of fresh herbs – tarragon, chervil, and chives – or just one favorite. Choose a couple of different kinds of apples too, one red, one green.

1/2 cup dry bread crumbs	2 apples, cored and cut
3 tbsp minced herbs	into 1/4-inch slices
4 skinless, boneless chicken	4 tsp vegetable oil
breast halves	2 tsp butter
1 egg white, beaten	2 tbsp dry white wine
salt and freshly ground pepper	fresh herb sprigs

Combine the crumbs and half of the herbs in a shallow dish. Flatten the chicken to 1/4-inch thickness and season with salt and pepper. Coat the chicken with the egg white, then the crumb mixture.

Heat 2 teaspoons of oil in a large, non-stick skillet over medium-high heat. Add 2 pieces of the chicken and sauté 1 to 2 minutes per side or until golden brown and cooked through. Remove to a warm platter and keep warm. Repeat with the remaining oil and chicken.

Heat the butter in the same skillet. Add the apples and sauté 1 minute. Stir in the wine and remaining herbs; simmer 1 or 2 minutes or until tender. Spoon over the chicken and garnish with herb sprigs.

Lamb Shanks in Red Wine

This recipe comes from Gwen Bassetti, a friend who raises sheep in Goldendale, Washington, high above the Columbia River Gorge. A Washington Merlot makes a good choice for both cooking and drinking as does an Oregon Pinot Noir. Washington State is now the second largest premium wine producer in the United States; Oregon is fourth.

4 meaty lamb shanks, sawed into 2-in lengths	salt
4 cloves garlic	freshly ground pepper
1 tsp fresh or dried thyme	1 rounded tbsp tomato paste
	2 cups dry red wine

Preheat oven to 325°F. Place each lamb shank on an 18-inch square of heavy-duty foil. Slice a garlic clove over each and sprinkle with $1/4$ tsp thyme and salt and pepper to taste. Shape the foil up around the shanks without closing it and place the packets in a large roasting pan. Dissolve the tomato paste in the wine and divide among the packets. Seal the packets tightly. Bake 1 $1/2$ to 2 $1/4$ hours or until tender. Transfer the lamb shanks and the sauce to shallow soup plates. Serve with Sheepherder's Bread (see p. 12).

Sautéed Wild Mushrooms

The forests and fields of the Northwest yield dozens of kinds of edible mushrooms. One of the most prized is the golden, trumpet-shaped chanterelle. In season from July to December, chanterelles can sometimes be found in grocery stores and farmers' markets.

---

1 lb chanterelles or other edible wild mushrooms	2–3 tbsp dry white wine
1–2 tbsp butter	2 tsp minced fresh summer savory or flat-leaf parsley
1 tbsp olive oil	salt
1–2 shallots, minced	freshly ground pepper

Wipe the mushrooms with a damp cloth. Tear the chanterelles into bite-size pieces or thinly slice other mushrooms. Heat the butter and oil in a large skillet over medium-high heat. Add the mushrooms and sauté 2 to 3 minutes or until they are cooked through and any liquid is reduced. Add the shallots and cook 2 minutes. Add the wine, herb and salt and pepper to taste; cover and cook 1 minute longer. Serve warm.

Berry Tartlets with Cream Cheese Filling

Perhaps it is the British influence, but afternoon tea is still an institution in British Columbia. The Murchie family, with head offices in Vancouver, has provided quality teas locally and by mail for close to a century. We like a steaming pot of Murchie's Extra Fancy Darjeeling with these little berry-topped cheesecake tarts. This recipe is a variation of one from Victoria's grand old Empress Hotel.

Pastry Shells:	Filling:
$1/3$ cup blanched almonds	8 oz cream cheese,
1 cup all-purpose flour	softened
$1/4$ cup sugar	$1/4$ cup sugar
$1/4$ tsp salt	1 egg, beaten
$1/2$ cup butter, softened	1 $1/2$ tsp lemon juice
2 tsp water	$3/4$ cup blueberries
$1/4$ tsp vanilla	$3/4$ cup raspberries

Grind the almonds in a food processor until fine. Add the flour, sugar, salt, and butter. Process until the mixture looks like fine, dry crumbs. Add the water and vanilla and process just until the dough forms a cohesive ball. Shape into a disk, wrap and chill at least 1 hour.

Preheat the oven to 375°F. Divide the dough into 12 equal pieces and press into 3-inch fluted tart pans. Place on a baking sheet and bake 20 minutes or until golden. Cool on a wire rack 10 minutes. Remove from pans and cool.

Beat the cream cheese, sugar, egg and lemon juice until light. Reduce the oven temperature to 350°F. Place pastry shells on a baking sheet and spoon in the cream cheese mixture. Arrange the berries decoratively on top. Bake 20 minutes or until set. Cool on a rack.

Cherry Clafouti

In the Limousin region of France, small tart cherries are used for this fruit custard, but in the Northwest we use fresh sweet cherries — either big, black Bings or the harder to find rosy-yellow Rainiers. If the cherry season is too short, try fresh blueberries or huckleberries.

3 cups sweet cherries, stemmed and pitted	²/₃ cup sifted all-purpose flour
butter	²/₃ cup sugar
1 ¹/₄ cups milk	¹/₄ tsp salt
3 eggs	powdered sugar
1 tbsp brandy or ³/₄ tsp vanilla	

Preheat the oven to 350°F. Spread the cherries in a buttered 2-quart baking dish. Blend the milk, eggs and brandy in a food processor or blender. Stir together the flour, sugar, and salt and sprinkle over the milk mixture. Process just until smooth. Pour the batter over the cherries. Bake about 45 minutes or until the top is puffed and brown and a knife inserted near the center comes out clean. Cool on a wire rack 10 minutes; it will deflate slightly. Sprinkle with powdered sugar and serve warm or at room temperature.

Northwest Blackberry Cobbler

Wild blackberries are a summertime treat throughout much of the Northwest. Growing in thorny tangles along rural roads and on vacant lots, ripe blackberries are pretty much there for the picking. My father-in-law, the champion berry picker of the family, has found sources near Qualicum Beach on Vancouver Island, in Clark Fork, Idaho, and on Seattle's Burke-Gilman Trail.

---

4 cups blackberries	2 tbsp sugar
1/2 cup sugar or to taste	1/4 tsp salt
1 tbsp flour	4 tbsp chilled butter,
1 tbsp butter	cut into bits
Biscuit Topping:	milk
1 cup all-purpose flour	cinnamon sugar
1 1/2 tsp baking powder	

Place the berries in a bowl. Combine the sugar and flour and stir into the berries. Pour into a buttered 2-quart baking dish and dot with butter.

Preheat the oven to 350°F. Sift the flour, baking powder, sugar, and salt into a bowl. Cut in the butter until crumbly. Stir in 1/3 cup milk, adding a little more if needed, and form into a ball. Knead gently a few times and roll out 1/2-inch thick on a floured surface. Cut into 4 circles and place over fruit. Brush them with milk and sprinkle with cinnamon sugar. Bake 30 minutes or until the fruit bubbles and the topping is browned. Serve warm with cream or vanilla ice cream, if desired.

Streusel-Topped Apple Cream Pie

Washington State is truly apple country. The irrigated Eastern part of the state is the biggest producer in the nation, but Western Washington, with its heavier rainfall, has many small orchards growing varieties such as Jonagold, Liberty, Spartan, and Gravenstein. For this apple pie (my husband's favorite) I use whatever kind looks the best and adjust the sugar accordingly.

1 9-inch unbaked pastry shell	4 cups chopped and peeled
1 cup light sour cream	cooking apples
1 egg, beaten	**Topping:**
1 tsp vanilla	$^1/_3$ cup packed brown sugar
$^1/_2 - ^3/_4$ cup sugar	1 tbsp all-purpose flour
1 tbsp all-purpose flour	1 tsp cinnamon
$^1/_8$ tsp salt	$^1/_4$ cup chilled butter

Preheat the oven to 375°F. Bake the pastry shell 7 minutes. Combine the sour cream, egg, and vanilla in a large bowl. Stir together the sugar, flour, and salt; mix with the sour cream mixture. Stir in the apples. Pour into the pastry shell. Bake 45 minutes.

To make the topping, combine the brown sugar, flour, and cinnamon in a bowl. Cut in the butter until crumbly. Sprinkle evenly over the pie and bake 15 minutes longer ar until a knife inserted near the center comes out clean. Serve warm or chilled.

Strawberry-Rhubarb Crisp

Our local strawberries, many of which carry names of mountains – Hood, Olympus, Shuksan, and, my favorite Rainier – are too fragile for shipping. So, for a few weeks in late spring, we enjoy them ourselves at their red-ripe best. To go with the strawberries, use either pink hothouse rhubarb or the larger red and green field-grown variety for this quick-to-make crisp.

2 cups sliced strawberries	¹/₂ tsp cinnamon
2 cups diced rhubarb	¹/₈ tsp cloves
³/₄ cup packed brown sugar	¹/₈ tsp salt
²/₃ cup rolled oats	4 tbsp chilled butter,
¹/₃ cup all-purpose flour	cut into bits

Preheat the oven to 350°F. Combine the strawberries and rhubarb in a 2-quart baking dish. Stir together the brown sugar, oats, flour, cinnamon, cloves, and salt in a bowl. Cut in the butter until crumbly. Sprinkle evenly over the fruit. Bake 40 minutes or until the fruit is bubbly and topping is lightly brown. Serve warm with vanilla ice cream, if desired.

Pear Tart with Caramel Sauce

This stunning Pear Tart is an adaptation of the one chef-owner Tom Douglas serves at the Dahlia Lounge in downtown Seattle. I've experimented with different pears and found that the firm, spicy Bosc holds its shape best.

Pastry:	Poached Pears:
1/4 cup almond paste	4 cups water
3 tbsp sugar	2 cups sugar
2 tbsp butter	1 vanilla bean, split and
2 egg yolks	scraped
1 (8–9 oz) sheet puff pastry,	4 firm-ripe Bosc pears
thawed	Caramel Sauce
	whipped cream and
	sliced almonds

(serves 8)

Combine the almond paste, sugar, butter, and egg yolks in a food processor; blend until smooth. Roll out pastry on a lightly floured surface to make a 15 x 10-inch rectangle. Cut into 8 pieces. Place on a baking sheet lined with parchment paper. Spoon some of the filling onto each piece and place the baking sheet in the freezer.

To poach the pears, combine the water, sugar, and vanilla bean in a large saucepan. Simmer 5 minutes. Halve, core, and peel the pears. Place in the syrup; cover and simmer gently 7 to 10 minutes or until pears are just cooked through. Drain on a paper-towel-lined cooling rack.

Preheat the oven to 425°F. Remove pastry from the freezer. Partially slice each pear to within 1/2 inch of the stem end. Fan out and lay the pear on top of the almond filling. Bake about 25 minutes or until golden. Cool 5 minutes. Or cool completely, then rewarm at 200°F about 10 minutes.

Place a tart on each plate and pour a little Caramel Sauce on top. Garnish with whipped cream and sliced almonds.

Caramel Sauce: This sauce is delicious drizzled over pound cake or ice cream as well as with the Pear Tarts. In summer, make a sundae using the peach topping (see p. 7) and vanilla ice cream.

³/₄ cup sugar	³/₄ cup heavy cream
3 tbsp water	I tbsp butter

(makes about I ¹/₄ cups)

Heat sugar and water in a heavy saucepan and stir until dissolved. Raise heat to high and boil without stirring until the liquid turns amber. Take from heat and pour in the cream. Stir in butter and return to heat. Cook and stir until smooth.

Chocolate Hazelnut Cake

At Sooke Harbour House on Vancouver Island, British Columbia, Sinclair and Fredrica Philip, the proprietors, grow their own fruits and vegetables, forage for wild edibles and catch fresh seafood just a few feet from the dining room. In this recipe Fredrica uses Northwestern hazelnuts in her grandmother's sensational chocolate cake.

8 oz semi-sweet chocolate	¹/₄ cup all-purpose flour
³/₄ cup unsalted butter	**Glaze:**
4 eggs, separated	3 oz semi-sweet chocolate
³/₄ cup sugar	¹/₄ cup unsalted butter
¹/₄ cup ground hazelnuts	¹/₄ cup toasted hazelnuts, coarsely chopped

(makes I 9-inch cake)

Grease and flour a 9-inch round cake pan and line the bottom with wax paper. Melt the chocolate and butter in the top of a double boiler; cool. Beat the egg yolks and gradually add the sugar, beating until thick. Stir in the chocolate then the hazelnuts. Sift the flour over the top and stir in.

Preheat the oven to 350°F. Beat the egg whites until stiff. Combine some of the whites with the chocolate mixture, then fold in the remaining whites until no streaks remain. Pour into the prepared pan. Bake 35 to 40 minutes or until the outside is firm but the center is underdone. Cool the cake in the pan 10 minutes, then invert on a rack and remove wax paper.

For the glaze, melt the chocolate and butter in the top of a double boiler. Spread over the cooled cake and top with the hazelnuts.

Biscotti

These twice-baked Italian style cookies are a Seattle favorite for dipping in Caffè Latte (see p. 59). Biscotti will keep for several weeks in an airtight container.

3 eggs	2 tsp anise seed
1 cup sugar	3 – 3 1/2 cups all-purpose flour
1/2 cup vegetable oil	1 1/2 tsp baking powder
2 tsp lemon peel	1/2 tsp salt
3 tbsp lemon juice	1 cup toasted hazelnuts,
1 tbsp vanilla	coarsely chopped
(makes about 45 cookies)	

In the large bowl of an electric mixer, beat the eggs and sugar together until light. Beat in the oil, lemon peel, and juice,

vanilla and anise seed. Stir together the dry ingredients and mix in with the nuts. The dough will be soft. Refrigerate at least 1 hour.

Preheat the oven to 325°F. Turn out the dough on a floured board and shape into 3 x 12-inch logs. Place on a greased cookie sheet and flatten to about ½ inch. Bake 25 to 30 minutes. Cool logs on a wire rack 10 minutes. Reduce the oven temperature to 300°F. Cut the logs diagonally into ½-inch slices. Place cut side down on baking sheets. Bake 15 minutes; turn and bake 5 minutes more or until dry. Cool on a wire rack.

Caffè Latte

Caffè Latte is the Italian term for espresso coffee with hot, steamed milk. But in Seattle, where espresso carts abound, lattes come short or tall (by the amount of milk), single, double or triple (amount of coffee), hot or iced, caf or decaf. Caffè mocha is a latte with a spoonful of chocolate syrup stirred in, whipped cream, and a sprinkle of cocoa powder.

---

1 shot (1–1 ½ oz) espresso or strong coffee
about ¾ cup low-fat or non-fat milk
sugar, optional
(serves 1)

Prepare a shot of espresso using an espresso machine and steam the milk until foamy and hot. Or brew double-strength coffee and beat the milk in a saucepan, whisking until hot and foamy. Pour the coffee into an 8-oz cup and pour the milk and foam over the top. Stir in sugar if desired.

Index